NETBALL F BEGINNERS TO PRO

Ultimate Guide to Rules, Techniques, Strategy, Position Play, Fitness Training, Skill Development, Drills, Coaching Tips, and Sportsmanship for Players and Coaches

BEN G. ELSTON

COPYRIGHT © 2023 BY BEN G. ELSTON

All rights reserved. No part of this publication may be reproduced, distributed, or transmitted in any form or by any means, including photocopying, recording, or other electronic or mechanical methods, without the prior written permission of the publisher, except in the case of brief quotations embodied in critical reviews and certain other noncommercial uses permitted by copyright law.

- CHAPTER ONE 5
  - INTRODUCTION TO NETBALL 5
    - A SYNOPSIS OF NETBALL HISTORY ...7
    - Netball Tools and Court Setup 9
    - Netball Roles and Positions 11
    - Fundamental Principles and Goals 15
- CHAPTER TWO 18
  - FUNDAMENTAL NETBALL SKILLS 18
    - Shooting Methods 23
    - DEFENSIVE ABILITIES AND MARKING 27
- CHAPTER THREE 31
  - NETBALL OFFENSE STRATEGIES 31
    - Making Room for Movement 34
  - TIMING AND PLACEMENT...................37
    - Fast Transitions and Breaks 39
- CHAPTER FOUR 45

DEFENDING TECHNIQUES IN NETBALL 45

> Deflections and Interceptions 51
>
> Teaming up twice and trapping 53
>
> Transitioning from Rebounding to Attacking 55

CHAPTER FIVE 59

GAME TACTICS IN NETBALL 59

> Center Pass Techniques 64
>
> Dealing with Tense Situations 66
>
> Adjusting to the Opponent's Strategies 68

CHAPTER SIX 72

NETBALL FITNESS AND TRAINING 72

> Routines for Warm-Up and Cool-Down 73

Exercises for Strength and Conditioning 76
Practice Your Quickness and Agility 79
Mental Focus and Preparation 81
THANK YOU 85

CHAPTER ONE
INTRODUCTION TO NETBALL

A quick-moving team sport called netball that incorporates aspects of handball, basketball, and soccer. Although men's netball is becoming more and more popular, women and girls still play it the majority of the time. The focus on collaboration, strategy, and accurate passing in the game defines it. The stimulating and competitive environment of netball challenges players' dexterity, coordination, and decision-making abilities.

Two teams of seven players each compete in the team sport of netball. The game's goal is to score points by passing the ball through the goalpost of the opposing team. Each player on the court is assigned a particular position and function, and the court is divided into thirds. The players are given predetermined sections of the court to play in and are given movement restrictions. Netball is a highly strategic and dynamic sport because it places a great focus on passing, placement, and teamwork.

A SYNOPSIS OF NETBALL HISTORY

Basketball, which was created in the late 19th century by Dr. James Naismith, is where netball's roots may be found. A modified version of basketball was used to create the game, which was intended to be played indoors and mostly by women. With some rules modified to fit female players' physical characteristics and preferred playing styles, netball was created to meet their demands.

The rules changed throughout time as the game gained popularity in many nations. The International Federation of Netball Associations (IFNA), currently known as the International Netball Federation (INF), was established in 1960 with the goal of regulating the sport's growth internationally. Since then, netball has developed into one of the most popular and viewed women's sports in the world.

Netball Tools and Court Setup

Netball requires little in the way of equipment, making it available to a variety of players. A netball, which is smaller than a basketball but a little lighter, and goalposts at either end of the court are required pieces of equipment.

Court Design

A rectangular netball court is divided into thirds and has a rectangular shape. The court measures 15.25 meters wide by 30.5 meters long. Several lines, including the center circle, transverse lines, goal circles, and shooting circles, are used to mark it.

The game starts with a center pass in the center of the court, or the center circle. Until the whistle is blown, players from both teams must remain outside the center circle.

Transverse Lines: During certain parts of the game, these lines are utilized to limit where specific players can travel by dividing the court into thirds.

Goal Circles: The goalposts are situated in these semicircular areas at each end of the court. In certain circumstances, only specified players are permitted to enter the goal circle.

Shooting Circles: Attacking players try to score goals in the shooting circles, which are inside the goal circles.

Netball Roles and Positions

There are seven different positions in netball, each with a unique set of duties and responsibilities on the court. Attackers and defenders are the two groups that these positions fall under.

Positions for Attacking:

Goal Shooter (GS): The main responsibility of the goal shooter is to score goals. They position themselves inside the shooting circle to receive passes and make precise shots while collaborating closely with the goal attack to create scoring possibilities.

Goal Attack (GA): This tactic mixes playmaking and goal scoring. By making passes, opening up space, and occasionally attempting shots, they aid the goal shooter.

The wing attack (WA) is in charge of supplying the ball to the shooting circle. They are essential in creating plays, keeping possession, and helping the attackers.

Defense Strategies:

The goalkeeper's main responsibility is to stop the opposition team's goal shooter from scoring. For the purpose of blocking shots and regaining possession of the ball, they must use their height, quickness, and defensive prowess.

Goal Defense (GD): The objective of goal defense is to thwart the offensive plays of the opposing side and stop the goal attack from scoring. Together with the goalie, they exert pressure and induce turnovers.

Wing Defense (WD): The primary function of the wing defense is to reduce the impact of the wing attack on the game. They concentrate on intercepting passes, carefully pursuing the opposition, and moving the ball from defense to attack.

The team's pivot, the center (C), serves both defensive and offensive purposes. They take possession of the ball at the center pass and are in charge of passing to teammates, keeping possession, and managing the tempo of the game.

Fundamental Principles and Goals

Basic Guidelines:

- Players must rotate on one foot while gripping the ball and not move until they pass.
- After receiving the ball, you have three seconds to pass it on.
- Except while attempting to intercept passes, players are not permitted to make physical contact with opponents. This regulation encourages non-contact play.

- A player must choose a landing foot after catching the ball. The opposite foot can then pivot after that.

Purposes:

Netball's main goal is to score more goals than the other side by passing the ball through its goalpost. Teams work to open up passing lanes, move the ball well, and take advantage of scoring opportunities. Teams try to induce mistakes, intercept passes, and stop their opponents from scoring when playing defense.

In conclusion, netball is a fascinating sport that needs extraordinary agility, collaboration, and strategic thinking. Netball continues to enthrall viewers and empower players all around the world thanks to its rich history, developing rules, and variety of player positions. Netball is a popular and enduring sport that highlights the strength and abilities of its competitors due to the dynamic aspect of the game, the camaraderie it develops, and the excitement of competition.

CHAPTER TWO

FUNDAMENTAL NETBALL SKILLS

To succeed in the sport of netball, one needs a solid foundation of essential abilities. Players need these abilities in order to engage effectively in all facets of the game, from passing and catching to shooting and defending. Acquiring these abilities improves a player's effectiveness while also helping the team as a whole. Let's examine the crucial netball fundamental skills:

Passing Procedures

In netball, passing is an essential ability since it promotes ball movement, generates scoring opportunities, and aids in maintaining possession. Precision, timing, and knowledge of your teammates' positions are all necessary for effective passing. In netball, numerous passing strategies are employed:

In netball, the chest pass is the most popular type of pass. Using a firm wrist flick, push the ball in the direction of your partner while holding it with both hands at chest height. Aim for a chest pass to your teammate that is accurate and direct.

Bounce Pass: To execute a bounce pass, you must bounce the ball in the direction of your teammate. In crowded sections of the court or under the arms of defenders, it is helpful. The ball should be bounced low and forcefully enough to hit the target.

The overhead pass, also referred to as a lob pass, is helpful for getting the ball over the heads of defenders. Holding the ball above your head with both hands, release it with a slight backspin. Longer distances benefit from the use of this pass.

Passing the ball against your shoulder while flicking your wrist to release it is known as the "Shoulder Pass." It comes in handy for making rapid, short-distance passes when you need to switch the play's direction.

Taking the Shot

As it affects how well a team can hold possession and switch from defense to attack, catching is just as crucial as passing. Focus, timing, and hand-eye synchronization are essential for effective catching techniques. The following are some crucial netball catching techniques:

Two-Handed Catch: Extend your arms and fingers towards the incoming ball, securing it with both hands. Position your hands to make a "W" shape, with your thumbs and index fingers forming the top points of the "W."

When the ball is coming at an angle that makes a two-handed catch difficult, a one-handed catch is used. Use your cupped hands to catch the ball by extending one arm in its direction.

Reach for the ball's highest point with your arms raised above your head to make a high catch. To hold the ball while maintaining control and balance, use your fingers and palms.

Low Catch: Get low and bend your knees to catch balls that are rolling or bouncing along the ground. Drop your arms and pick up the ball with your hands and fingers.

Shooting Methods

Since shooting is how teams win points in netball, it is the ultimate goal. A mix of technique, accuracy, and pressure-free calmness are necessary for shooting. The main netball shooting techniques are as follows:

The goal shooter (GS) is in charge of scoring goals that are near to the net. Their shooting side foot should be somewhat in front of them as they stand with their shoulders relaxed and their knees slightly bent. The non-shooting hand supports the ball from the side while the shooting hand is submerged beneath it. Release the ball with a backspin in a fluid motion, aiming for the middle of the hoop.

Goal Attack Technique: The goal attack (GA), which employs a similar technique to the goal shooter, frequently needs to shoot from midrange positions. They continue to use a similar shooting stance and technique that emphasizes accuracy and reliability.

Movement and Footwork

In netball, a player's ability to generate space, change directions, and maintain optimum positioning depends on their footwork and movement. To retain a non-contact style of play, the netball regulations set limitations on footwork. The following are some footwork maneuvers and techniques:

When a player catches the ball, they put one foot in the pivot position. The ball is not released until this foot lets go of the ground. Before passing or shooting, the other foot can pivot around the pivot foot to shift direction.

Lateral Movement: Players shift sideways while retaining their defensive or attacking stances, staying close to their opponent.

Dodging: To get around a defender and open up space, you need to quickly change directions. Players outmaneuver opponents by moving quickly and changing their speed.

Attacking players use the front cut to quickly change directions and advance toward the ball. It entails moving in the direction of the passer before quickly turning around to catch the ball.

DEFENSIVE ABILITIES AND MARKING

It takes strong defensive play and effective marking to stop the other side from scoring. A defensive player needs to be agile, well-positioned, and anticipatory. Here are some marking and defending strategies:

Interception: In order to intercept passes, players must study the game, anticipate their opponents' moves, and time their own movements to block the ball's route.

Man-to-Man Marking: Each defender in a man-to-man defense is given an opponent to closely mark. Staying between the opposition and the goalpost and applying pressure to impede their movements is the objective.

Instead of marking specific opponents, players in a zone defense defend regions of the court as a whole. The goal of this strategy is to restrict passing lanes and cause turnovers.

Blocking: Defenders use their body and arms to obstruct an opponent's view and keep them from efficiently passing or shooting.

Defenders work to get the rebound and regain control of the ball following a failed shot. In order to box out opponents, this involves placement, timing, and body alignment.

In conclusion, it is critical for players to learn the fundamentals of netball in order to succeed in this strategic and dynamic sport. These abilities not only improve individual performance but also the team's overall strategy, teamwork, and success. Honing these abilities enables players to significantly improve their team's performance and succeed on the netball court, whether it is through accurate passing, accurate shooting, agile footwork, or effective defense.

CHAPTER THREE

NETBALL OFFENSE STRATEGIES

In order to create scoring opportunities, keep possession, and outmaneuver the opposing defense, effective offensive methods are crucial in netball. A thorough understanding of offensive principles, movement, timing, and coordination are necessary for a well-coordinated attack. Let's examine the main offensive tactics used by teams to succeed in netball:

Attacking Ideas

An effective offensive strategy in netball is built on attacking ideas. These guidelines help players make wise choices, take advantage of opportunities, and play to their team's strengths. The following are some crucial attacking tenets:

Keep Possession: Maintaining possession of the ball is one of the main aims of an offensive strategy. To keep control, players should concentrate on making precise passes, preventing turnovers, and cooperating with one another.

Attacking players should pass the ball to open areas so they can move into favourable positions to receive it. This will attempt to penetrate the defense of the opposition. Opportunities to pass or shoot are created via penetration.

Ball Movement: To confuse the defender and expose gaps in their coverage, quick and precise ball movement is essential. To change the defense and open up spaces, players should combine short, fast passes with longer, smart plays.

choices and Support: Attacking players should constantly give the ball-carrier choices. This entails taking up positions in open areas, separating from defenders using feints, and keeping ideal passing angles.

Variation: Attacking plans should include a range of passes, movements, and plays to confuse the defense. By varying the play style, the defender is unable to predict movements and patterns.

Making Room for Movement

To undermine the defense of the opposition and create scoring opportunities, space and movement on the court are crucial. Attacking players must cooperate in order to trick the defense and locate open spaces. Here are some methods for making room for movement:

Off-the-Ball Movement: Players who are not in possession of the ball should move continuously to position themselves for passes. To confuse defenders, this entails cutting, dodging, and changing directions.

Attacking players should move out of the way of the ball carrier's intended movements or passes. By clearing the field, teammates can receive the ball in opportune locations and pass lanes can be opened up.

Blocking and screening: Players can set blocks or screens to obstruct defenders and provide room for their teammates. Effective screens that free up players for passes or shoots depend on timing and synchronization.

Triangle passing: Arranging players on the court in triangle formation improves passing choices and provides additional support. Players may move the ball across the court swiftly and locate open teammates by keeping proper spacing.

TIMING AND PLACEMENT

In order to execute successful offensive plays, timing and positioning are essential. The proper time to pass or move must be anticipated, and players must be aware of the movements of their teammates. Here is how offensive techniques utilize timing and positioning:

Timing of Passes: It's crucial to time passes so that the ball arrives when the player receiving it is prepared to collect it. Passing too soon or too late might result in errors or lost chances.

Attacking players can direct their teammates into open areas with lead passes. They can predict where a player will be and pass appropriately by being aware of their teammates' movements.

Front Positioning: When receiving passes, attacking players should try to place themselves in front of their defenders. In doing so, they can protect the ball and improve the angle of their next move.

Baseline Drives: To get closer to the goalpost, attacking players might drive along the baseline. This motion has the potential to deter opponents and open up passing lanes close to the goal circle.

Fast Transitions and Breaks

Taking advantage of a disjointed defense or swiftly switching from defense to offense are both examples of fast breaks and transitions. These tactics surprise the opposition and provide rapid scoring opportunities. Here is how quick transitions and breaks operate:

Rapid Transitions: The team quickly switches from defense to offensive after regaining possession of the ball. In order to surprise the defense, players should advance the ball swiftly up the court.

Players should search for an outlet pass as soon as they have the ball to begin the fast break. In order to take advantage of the defense's disorganization, the outlet pass needs to be precise and rapid.

Mismatch Exploitation: During transition, teams might spot and take advantage of defensive mismatches. The team can rapidly send the ball to a player who clearly has the advantage in terms of speed, placement, or size for a high-percentage scoring opportunity.

Attack Teamwork

An efficient attacking plan in netball is built on teamwork. To maximize their scoring potential, players must communicate, work together, and comprehend each other's talents and inclinations. Here are several ways where attack collaboration is essential:

On the court, players should communicate to signal where they want the ball to go, to call out plays, and to signal for passes. Making informed judgments and carrying out plays smoothly are made possible by effective communication.

Passing choices: Attacking players should give their teammates passing choices by carefully placing themselves. Multiple passing lanes provide the ball carrier with more options while lowering the chance of interceptions.

Player Roles: Each player in the attacking strategy is responsible for a particular task. Players will be in the best positions to contribute effectively if they are aware of these responsibilities and treat them with respect.

Making Decisions: Teamwork entails coming to a decision as a group based on how the game is progressing. Players should analyze the circumstances, weigh their options, and make choices that advance the group's goal as a whole.

In conclusion, attacking concepts, mobility, timing, transitions, and teamwork are important to offensive strategy in netball. Teams can generate scoring opportunities, keep possession, and keep the opposition on its toes by successfully utilizing these methods. Successful netball teams succeed not just in each player's individual abilities but also in their teamwork on the court. What makes netball an exciting and engrossing sport to watch and play is the dynamic interplay of attacking concepts and synchronized movements.

CHAPTER FOUR

DEFENDING TECHNIQUES IN NETBALL

In netball, defensive tactics are essential for stymieing the opposition's attack, regaining possession of the ball, and stopping them from scoring. A successful defensive strategy necessitates a firm grasp of defensive principles, positioning, foresight, and teamwork. Let's examine the primary defensive tactics used by teams to succeed in netball:

Defensive Guidelines

A successful defensive strategy in netball is built on defensive concepts. These guidelines help players mark opponents, challenge passes, and put pressure on the ball. Following are some crucial defensive guidelines:

Marking: To restrict an opponent's range of motion and passing choices, one must closely protect them. To maintain their position in front, players should position themselves between the opposition and the goalpost and employ dynamic footwork.

To make interceptions and turnovers, it is crucial to anticipate the opponent's movements and passes. Defenders should analyze the situation, anticipate passes, and take up advantageous positions to block passing lanes.

Coordination of switches, assignments, and strategies among defenders depends on effective communication. Switches should be called, teammates should be informed of opponents' moves, and assistance should be given.

Keeping adversaries from roaming freely about the court is known as containment. Defenders can reduce their opponent's options by using lateral movements, body placement, and well-timed challenges.

Patience: Defenders should use patience and refrain from lunging or overcommitting, which might provide gaps that their adversaries can take advantage of. Defenders can wait for the ideal opportunity to intercept or challenge if they maintain their composure.

Defense Types: Zone vs. Man-to-Man

Based on the strengths of their players, the tactics of their opponents, and the circumstances of the game, teams might decide between zone and man-to-man defense. Each strategy has benefits and drawbacks:

Man-to-Man Defense: Each defender is given an opponent to carefully mark in man-to-man defense. Strong footwork, communication, and individual marking skills are necessary for this strategy. Man-to-man defense may put tremendous pressure on opponents and sabotage their plays.

In zone defense, defenders keep an eye on particular areas of the court rather than individual opponents. With this strategy, the goal is to obstruct passing lanes, induce turnovers, and reduce scoring opportunities. To properly cover broad regions, zone defense involves cooperation, communication, and swift movements.

Deflections and Interceptions

In netball, interceptions and deflections are crucial elements of an effective defensive plan. These moves break up the opposition's passing and shooting flow, giving the defending team the ball back. Interceptions and deflections operate as follows:

Defenders should anticipate the ball's trajectory and position themselves wisely to intercept passes by reading the play. This entails reading play patterns, interpreting body language, and making pass predictions.

Interceptions call for precise timing. To have the best chance of blocking the pass, defenders should move as soon as the ball is launched.

Defenders can try to deflect the ball by placing their hand or body in its path if an interception is not possible. The accuracy of the pass can be compromised by deflections, which also provide the opposing team an opportunity to take possession.

Teaming up twice and trapping

Defensive tactics like double teaming and trapping include concentrating on a single opponent to put pressure on them and force mistakes. These tactics call for communication, fast movements, and cooperation between the defenders. Double teaming and trapping operate as follows:

Double teaming: When two defenders double team, they concentrate their attention on the same opponent. This tactic tries to apply so much pressure that it overwhelms the opposition, reduces their passing choices, and results in turnovers.

Trapping: A more aggressive kind of double teaming is trapping. It entails strategically closing in on an opponent to put them in a position where they have few choices for passing or movement.

Transitioning from Rebounding to Attacking

Securing control of the ball after a missed shot is known as rebounding, which is an important defensive technique. Effective rebounding allows the defensive team to switch to offense and denies the opponent any second-chance opportunities. Rebounding and switching to an assault operate as follows:

Boxing Out: Players box out their opponents before rebounding. In order to put some distance between the opponent and the ball, one must use body placement. Players can improve their chances of getting the rebound by boxing out.

Timing and Positioning: Rebounders should coordinate their jump with the trajectory of the ball. To ensure they secure the rebound, players can jump vertically or reach out with their arms.

Outlet Pass: After securing the rebound, the player should quickly make an outlet pass to initiate the attack. The outlet pass needs to be precise and aimed at a teammate who is well-positioned to move the ball up the court.

Fast Breaks: Players should rapidly switch to attacking by moving the ball up the court after securing the rebound. Before the defense has a chance to set up, this fast break strategy throws the opposition off guard and offers scoring opportunities.

In summary, netball defensive techniques combine concepts, positioning, anticipation, and collaboration. Teams can thwart an opponent's attack, retrieve possession, and limit scoring possibilities by properly marking opponents, making interceptions, applying pressure, and completing defensive plays. Netball success requires a well-planned and smart defensive approach since it supports the team's offensive efforts and helps create a balanced and competitive game.

CHAPTER FIVE
GAME TACTICS IN NETBALL

In netball, game tactics refer to the tactical choices and moves that teams make to gain an advantage over their opponents, manage the game's pace, and accomplish their goals. A combination of set plays, tactical posture, and the capacity for adaptation to various circumstances and adversaries make up effective game tactics. Let's examine the primary game strategies used by teams to succeed in netball:

Fixed Plays and Approaches

Set plays are pre-planned strategies used by teams to set up scoring opportunities or manage the game's tempo. These plays call for precision execution and player cooperation. Here are some typical set plays and netball tactics:

Plays known as "inbounds" are utilized when bringing the ball back into play after it has left the bounds. In order to advance the ball down the court and create passing opportunities, players position themselves tactically.

Screening: Screens are part of set plays that are used to position players for a shot or a pass. In order to block a defender and provide room for a teammate to receive the ball, a player sets a screen.

Isolation Plays: An isolation play pits a skilled player against their opponent in a one-on-one matchup. This tactic is frequently employed to take advantage of a good matchup and generate a scoring chance.

Overload: To gain a numerical advantage and open passing lanes, the overload strategy involves concentrating players on one side of the court. This can result in efficient ball movement and confound the opposition.

Fake Passes: In these plays, one player pretends to pass to another while actually rapidly passing to the first. A chance for an open pass to another player is presented by the fake pass, which attracts defenders to the intended recipient.

Use of the Shooting Circle

Scoring opportunities are created in the shooting circle, therefore successful tactics here can have a big impact on a team's performance. The shooting circle can be used to your team's benefit in the following ways:

Positional Play: To open up paths for passes and shooting possibilities, attackers should place themselves strategically within the shooting circle. This entails making quick cuts, changing directions, and being mindful of the positions of the defenders.

Feeding the Shooter: The attacking players outside the shooting circle should coordinate to pass the ball to the shooters in a precise and timely manner. To do this, you must think of passing angles and pay attention to the shooter's positioning.

Rebounds and Second Chances: Attackers should be prepared to grab offensive rebounds following a failed shot. Players can set themselves up for tap-ins and rebounds to give their team a second chance to score.

Center Pass Techniques

The center pass, which establishes the tone for the team's attacking play, is a vital moment in the game. Several tactics can be used by teams to increase the efficiency of their center passes:

Quick Transition: The team with the center pass should strive to make the transition from defense to offensive as quickly as possible after the other team scores. This throws the opposition off guard and makes it possible for rapid breaks.

Multiple Passing alternatives: Players should provide the player receiving the center pass with a variety of pass alternatives. Players do this by carefully placing themselves around the center circle to offer alternatives on various parts of the court.

To provide the ball carrier clear passing choices, players should shift and create space right after the center pass. The defense's capacity to anticipate passes and apply pressure is interfered with by this movement.

Dealing with Tense Situations

The opponent's tactics, a tight defense, or the game's score can all create pressure circumstances. Successful teams maintain composure under duress and use certain strategies:

Quick ball movement can assist players in finding open passing lanes and relieving defensive pressure when they are under defensive pressure. To keep possession, this calls for making quick, accurate passes.

Quickly changing directions can open up space and frighten off opponents. To shift their trajectory and escape pressure, players can use dodges, pivots, and lateral movements.

Support and Communication: When a teammate is under pressure, players should communicate with them and offer their assistance. Players can release pressure and advance the ball by shouting for the ball and offering passing options.

Adjusting to the Opponent's Strategies

A fundamental characteristic of successful netball teams is adaptability. Different methods and techniques could be used by opponents to undermine your team's performance. A team can adjust to an opponent's tactics in the following ways:

Scouting: Through scouting, teams can research the playstyles and tendencies of their opponents. Teams can use this knowledge to predict their opponents' moves and modify their own strategies as necessary.

Flexible Defense: Teams should be ready to transition between zone and man-to-man defense as necessary if the opposition employs successful tactics. This flexibility can throw off the opponent's strategy.

Counterattacking: By reversing an opponent's strategy, teams can take advantage of their weaknesses. For instance, if the opposition plays a defensive strategy that is too aggressive, quick passes and fast breakaway can catch them off guard.

On-court communication is essential for quickly adjusting to an opponent's strategies. Players should advise their teammates of an opponent's movements, positioning, and strategy.

In conclusion, netball game tactics cover a wide range of tactics, plays, and flexibility. To outsmart opponents, create scoring opportunities, and keep control of the game, you must use effective strategies. Successful netball teams combine skillful execution with strategic decision-making, whether it's deploying set plays, maximizing the potential of the shooting circle, adapting to different scenarios, or combating opponents' strategies. On the court, elite netball players and teams can be identified by their capacity to read the game, make tactical adjustments, and work together as a unit.

CHAPTER SIX

NETBALL FITNESS AND TRAINING

The performance, endurance, and overall success of players on the court are all influenced by fitness and training, which are essential components of netball. Warm-up and cool-down routines, cardiovascular conditioning, strength and conditioning drills, agility and quickness training, and mental preparation are all included in a thorough training program. Let's examine each of these elements in more detail to comprehend their significance and how they help develop a well-rounded netball player:

Routines for Warm-Up and Cool-Down

Warm-up: Before participating in any physical activity, including netball, a suitable warm-up is necessary. It increases blood flow, warms up muscles, and improves joint flexibility to get the body ready for the workout or game that will soon be played. Dynamic stretches, light running, and functional motions that resemble netball-specific movements, like arm swings, squats, and lateral movements, could all be included in a standard warm-up regimen. Players are mentally ready for the challenges ahead thanks to the warm-up's progressive increase in heart rate.

Cool-down: Following vigorous exercise, it's important to follow a cool-down program to progressively lower heart rate, avoid muscle pain, and speed up recovery. The body may adapt from high intensity to rest with the aid of static stretching, deep breathing, and moderate movements during a cool-down. Additionally, cooling down helps reduce muscular stiffness and increases general flexibility, both of which are crucial for avoiding injuries.

Cardiovascular Exercise

Cardiovascular fitness, commonly referred to as cardio conditioning, is essential for netball players. The ability of players to maintain a high level of activity during the game is enhanced by a healthy cardiovascular system. Running, cycling, swimming, and high-intensity interval training (HIIT) are a few examples of exercises that can be used for cardiovascular training. As a result, players are better able to perform well during the quick-paced and physically demanding game of netball. These exercises also aid to boost lung capacity, oxygen delivery to muscles, and general stamina.

Exercises for Strength and Conditioning

Building muscle strength, power, and general body stability requires strength and conditioning activities.

Jumping, pivoting, and sprinting are just a few of the motions that netball players must perform, all of which exert a heavy burden on their muscles and joints. Strength training helps athletes perform better, prevent injuries, and improve their capacity for quick movements.

Resistance Training: Including movements like squats, lunges, deadlifts, and plyometrics in your routine can help you build leg and core strength. These movements improve players' capacity to jump, land, and change directions by using the main muscular groups utilized in netball.

Strengthening the core is essential for retaining equilibrium, stability, and effective movement on the court. Strengthening the stomach and lower back muscles with core workouts like planks, Russian twists, and leg lifts improves overall athleticism.

Upper Body Strength: Passing, shooting, and guarding all require strong upper bodies. Push-ups, pull-ups, and shoulder presses are exercises that help build the arms, shoulders, and back muscles, which improves a player's overall strength and performance.

Practice Your Quickness and Agility

For netball players, agility and quickness training are essential because the sport calls for swift changes in direction, acceleration, and deceleration. Players' capacity to respond quickly to opponent movements and take advantage of scoring opportunities is improved by developing agility and quickness.

Exercises that improve agility include zigzags, cone drills, and lateral shuffles. These drills help athletes become more adept at lateral movement and quickly changing direction.

Speed training: The goal of speed training is to increase sprinting speed. To improve acceleration and top-end speed, athletes run shuttle runs, intervals, and short sprints.

Reaction Training: Players' reaction times and decision-making abilities are tested through drills that are part of reaction training. Players who receive this kind of instruction learn to read their opponents' intentions and react appropriately.

Mental Focus and Preparation

Focus and mental preparation are equally crucial aspects of netball training. The game's mental component affects decision-making, focus, and calm under pressure.

Visualization: Mental rehearsal of scenes, actions, and plays is a technique used in visualization. Players can increase their confidence and their comprehension of the game by visualizing successful plays.

Positive Self-Talk: Using positive self-talk to cultivate a positive mindset helps people feel more confident and self-assured. Positive affirmations can assist athletes maintain their focus and fortitude in trying circumstances.

Techniques like mindfulness and relaxation exercises can help players manage stress, remain in the present moment, and regulate worry. Mental clarity and emotional control are enhanced by deep breathing and meditation exercises.

Setting goals is important because it keeps athletes motivated and dedicated to their training program. Goals may be connected to accomplishments in performance, skill growth, or physical fitness.

In conclusion, being physically fit and receiving proper training are crucial to being a good netball player. The body is better prepared for physical exercise and recovers faster with warm-up and cool-down activities. A player's total performance, endurance, and capacity to flourish on the netball court are influenced by cardiovascular conditioning, strength and conditioning exercises, agility training, and mental preparation. Players are well-prepared to handle the rigors of the sport, make wise judgments, and execute plays efficiently when training is approached holistically and includes both physical and mental components.

THANK YOU

Printed in Great Britain
by Amazon